Alive

KARA DOBIAS

ALIVE

First Edition 2024

Published by: Kara Dobias

Book Design by: Kristina Conatser | Capturedbykcdesigns.com

Cover Image by: Maurice Shriqui

ISBN-13: 979-8-218-45655-9

For the deeply feeling souls — those finding their way back to their light.
You are enough. You are so loved.

Thank you for being here.

Contents

Preface

WHAT DOES IT MEAN TO BE ALIVE? Surely, this is a question too great for any one person to answer, and I would never claim that I could, alone, but I will put my faith in poets to bring us collectively closer. In poetry, I have found the nuance of this life freely expressed, and it is through our shared vulnerability that we find humanity.

I wrote this collection of poems during one of the most challenging seasons of my life—a season full of changes that made me feel powerless and caused me to question my self-definition. But as I began to find comfort through writing, I realized I had a choice. I could continue to be consumed by grief or be the framer of my story.

This book became an act of reclamation, a way for me to look loss in the face and say, "There will always be parts of me you cannot take," because even when hardship threatens our strength, we must find a way to continue moving forward.

The more that I wrote, the more I healed, never seeking to romanticize my pain but to alchemize it. I freed myself of expectation, for once not worrying about the opinions of others but instead shifting my focus to being unabashedly honest, allowing myself to surrender to the glorious messiness that comes with being human. I collected moments from my life like secrets tucked between journal pages to capture the ephemeral, preserving what was beautiful and processing what was not. Themes of identity, grief, and love all began to emerge in a body of work that started to feel much bigger than myself as I recognized the universality of my feelings. As a result, my writing shifted from a mere personal endeavor to something meant for anyone else who may need it. By sharing these moments from my life, I hope we can recognize ourselves in one another and, in turn, feel a little less alone. Sometimes, finding the right words at the right time can make all the difference.

In many ways, this book is a story of rebirth—a meditation on the lives we outgrow to become who we are meant to be and a reflection on the freedom to be found in letting go. The experiences and relationships I recount throughout these pages changed me irrevocably, and though not always easy, I am thankful for how I have grown.

We are here to live fully alive—this means acknowledging both the good and bad, knowing that we are not defined by or lesser for the struggles we face, as we will make it through our worst days. I hope my words are a reminder that to be alive is so achingly, terribly, beautiful.

Alive

What makes you feel most alive?
I don't think enough people
dare to ask this question,
let alone answer it.

I find myself in the unconventional.
I don't know if this makes me ungrounded,
but I like flirting with daydreams.

I'm inspired by those who dare to see
the impossible.
Maybe some would say that I
lack a sense of reality,
but I would counter that they just aren't
paying attention.

I'm the kind of person
who will try to find beauty in everything.
Quite frankly, I don't see the point
in being any other way.
I want to surround myself with art and music.
I want to dance away my pain and console myself with prose.
You see, I'm doing it even now.

I've tried to walk a straight path before,
but my destiny has laughed at the notion that
my life could possibly be linear.
I don't always conform to the status quo—
in fact, I'm getting more comfortable with
coloring outside of the lines.
Though some would try to pull me back inside.

I recognize that this may be a lonely life for me,
one fraught with chasing the next big thing—
the next rush of emotion,
the next burst of creativity.
But I've resigned myself to the reality
that, to be authentically me,
I cannot be anything but vulnerable—
sometimes painfully so.

Sometimes I feel misunderstood.
Even by those who claim to love me the most.
I cannot explain it—
I'm at once altogether here,
entirely present,
but simultaneously projecting myself into a future
that may never come to pass.

In short, I think a lot.
About everything.
All the time.

Like how this moment is fleeting and I'll never be as I am now, again.
Or how I fear losing those I love most
because loss seems to be my closest confidant.
I love fiercely, and I know that can be scary.
I wish I knew what that felt like—
to be on the receiving end of my love.
I'm still learning how to fill my cup.

To be alive is so achingly, terribly, beautiful.

Becoming

What if we were more honest about our mess,
and the phrase, *it's okay to not be okay,*
was not just something said
but truly meant?

I want to bask in my undoing.
Baptize me over and over so that I may meet
each new version of myself, renewed.

I will not lie to you.
The person you meet today may not exist
a year from now.
And isn't that beautiful?
Isn't that growth?

Complacency is a death sentence.
I will not stop living before it's my time to
meet the grave.

Join me in this journey of self-discovery.
I will never judge you in your process,
and I hope that you will grant me the same grace.

Let us learn from one another.
Let us never shy away from the pieces
we must live in before we become
whole.

Find Your Way

How do you conceptualize a loss
that isn't physical?
How do you describe losing all-knowingness
of a person still here
in body?

Maybe our humanity is so fragile as to be lost when we
lose our self-definition.

The importance of grounding
cannot be overstated.
To know oneself is to be anchored in
mind,
body,
and spirit.

I've witnessed the dissolution
of identity;
I've seen depression and anxiety
claim a life not yet over.

How can I reach through the fog?
How can I get through to you?
Do I even have that power?

Maybe it's the savior instinct in me,
but I'm not strong enough to
carry us both.

There's something to be said about
self-accountability.

I hope you find your way
back to me.

Beautiful Undoing

I don't want your feigned laughter or
plastered-on smile.
Your eyes reveal you, my dear.
They are the windows to your soul.

I want you here,
in your beautiful undoing.
You don't need my permission to cry.
Let the pain cascade down your cheeks;
you needn't hold onto it anymore.

We all have struggles we feel
compelled to hide.

Eleven

The first time I recognized depression
as a feeling
was when I was eleven.

Standing at a Christmas tree lighting,
surrounded by merriment,
but feeling a void of sadness
within me.

Tonight, at twenty-five, I watch as children
line the streets,
waiting for Santa to arrive on a
decked-out firetruck.
All I Want for Christmas Is You starts to play
amidst the sound of sirens.
The man in red shouts greetings of
Merry Christmas.
A little girl screams, *Hi Santa!*
with childhood innocence,
eliciting a reply of,
How old are you?

The first time I recognized depression
as a feeling
was when I was eleven.

Still Here

Was it a chemical imbalance that sent my mind into overdrive?
I felt like a ghost in my hometown,
walking streets I knew without connection.

It starts slowly, it seems.
The heaviness creeps in,
almost like the chill of night upon the arrival of dusk.
You start to have the thought, *"What if I wasn't here?"*
"Would it even matter?"
"Would they even care?"

You start to withdraw.
You don't respond to that invite;
stop posting on your socials.
There's so much noise, ***it's almost too easy*** to get lost—
to silence your
voice.

Everyone is so busy that they don't notice.
They write it off as you being involved in
your own life.
What they don't realize is that all you can think about is
ending yours.
So when the thoughts enter,
their gravity doesn't even hit you
because you've already begun ***to remove yourself from the narrative.***
You've seen that even in your absence,
Life
Goes
On.

Now what you can't see is that
You
Do
Matter.
Your life *does* add value to the world,
and when you finally **come back to life**—
revive yourself from the pits of your mental hell—
you start to see how your words carry weight
and how your empathy makes other lonely souls
feel less alone.

You rediscover the word *"gratitude"*
because you are thankful **you are still here.**
Here to laugh with your best friends until your breath is heaving
and there are tears in your eyes.
Here to fall in love for the first time with someone who truly sees you
and wants more,
not less.
Here to watch so many more sunrises and sunsets,
cap nights with a glass of wine, and indulge in
deep conversation.

You realize that you were never your pain;
it was just a teacher—
a guiding light back to yourself
despite the rockiness of the journey.
And you vow to live for every new moment,
to fight for the life and love you deserve,
because you realize:
You've been born anew.

Kaleidoscope

When I was little,
my grandparents kept a kaleidoscope airplane
on a side table in their
sunken 1960s living room.

I used to love to look through the viewfinder,
rotating the toy ever so slightly
until it produced what seemed to be an infinity
of colorful patterns.
I could lose myself in the little galaxy it created.

At 25, I think of how life resembles a kaleidoscope,
with the pieces of our lives in constant motion,
bringing a colorful dynamism
to our worlds.

But unlike when I was a child,
the chaos of these moving parts scares me.

Sometimes I want to apologize for my mess.
I worry that maybe I don't make sense
and my life looks strange from the outside—
not easily tracked or categorized.

I hope one day to bring my scattered pieces together
to create a fully realized vision,
so that I may be someone worth admiring.
I'm learning that maybe that just takes time.

I used to think that age would bring more order
to my understanding of the world.

Why, then, do I always have more questions than answers?

The truth is, I'm finding that it would better suit me
to revisit the child with her eye on the kaleidoscope,
for she understood surrendering.

Found

I found myself in bars,
laughing with friends,
forgetting my manners in Times Square
when I laugh so hard, I almost fall over.

I found myself cloaked in a suit jacket and red lipstick,
punctuating sentences about my trauma because I'm proud to say that
I'm starting to move past it.
That is to say, I'm growing through the pain.

I found myself in coffee at 10 p.m.
when the park-keeper is making his rounds
and I'm nestled with friends at a table,
looking up at the skyscrapers, yet feeling infinite
instead of small.

I found myself in the beauty of now
and realizing I just paid for overpriced drinks.
But you can't put a price on
a night out with people who tell you
they're proud of how far you've come and that your personality is beautiful.

I found myself when I stopped trying to fit everyone else's narrative
and started
creating
my
own.

I am here.
I am home in this body again.

Timelines

I spent some time in art school
during the autumn, when I was eighteen.
Countless hours were given
to putting charcoal on paper
for figure studies.
I know I can turn us into art.
The poetry pours with prose
to trace our image,
and I want a reminder that time cannot take.

I take your hand, mid-November
in this city that cements secrets
to show you the campus.
Walking through empty, sunlit studios,
we breathe new life into
my old memories.
There is an intimacy to crossing timelines
when a past and present become intertwined.

Here, we become picture proof for the first time—
a background of Brooklyn brick;
a smile you could cosign
because I haven't been this happy in a while.
It feels just like a scene
I would orchestrate in my mind
all the times I walked these
same streets
alone.
For all that time has taken,
I am grateful that it's given me,
you.

Later, when I leave you
to catch my train, I look at our photo.
A forehead kiss, your arm around me,
and the secret kept silently on my lips—
I hope you choose to stay.

Burn

Sometimes I am like fire—
feared but revered for its beauty;
unapologetic to its capacity for consumption;
burning with brilliance;
dancing with reckless abandon.

And while I burned the life I knew,
I found you in the embers—
a catalyst I hoped wouldn't lead to casualties.

A Little Less Alone

I told him, *I'm afraid.*
Though I've felt it,
I never said it out loud.
Scared by my ambition,
scared that it won't work out—
that I'm not as good or prepared
as I'd like to think.

And he told me,
You're more than capable.
Think of all you've accomplished so far.

So we lived in this moment,
and I felt
a little less
alone.

Atlas

Sometimes I get distracted,
and my thoughts only come to me
in poems
because I'm feeling the weight of the world—
like Atlas holding the heavens.

I'm trying to hold it all together because
I'm a strong woman.
Right?
I'm a strong woman.
That's what I tell myself.

But some days I wish
I could lighten my load.
Let go of all that isn't mine
to hold.
I'm a self-assigned savior who needs saving.
What would you say if I asked you to
shoulder the burden?

You once told me you believe
I hold the universe in me.
But Atlas wasn't given his job for his strength.
It was a punishment to be forced to hold that weight.
Must we bend so far that we eventually break?

Life likes to test these limits, it seems.

But I want to be praised past my productivity.
I'm worthy beyond my workload.
Is it too much to ask to simply,
be?

I'm a strong woman.
But today I will focus on
upholding the universe
of me.

Maybe I've always been a live wire liability—
electricity when you touched me.

How I Love You

You never opened your sunroof
while driving in the city.
Let me paint you
a new perspective.

I live in colors
you've never seen.
It can be overwhelming, I know.

But we found understanding
in our shared vulnerability.
That's all I've ever wanted—
for you to let me see you.

Tell me about your namesake
and the streets that connect you
with your past.

It's okay; I'm here to listen.
I'll hold your hand while you do.
We fit together just right.

To realize the nuance of love
is to see that there are a hundred ways
to show you care.

This is how I love you.

Muse

That I would bend language
to lessen the space
between us, there is no question.
But how many love poems
would it take to make you
stay with me?

Message in a Bottle

I'm standing on the shoreline,
the wind whipping my hair,
warning me to turn back.
But I can't see the storm clouds.
Everything has been hazy since
you.

I've just penned a letter
explaining how much
you mean to me.
The ink might as well be blood because I bore
so
deep
into
myself
to find the words.

I place it in a bottle,
seal it with a kiss,
and let the waves lap it up.

I speak to the ocean, and I tell her
to carry my message to you.
She crashes into the rocks and promises that she'll do her best.
But promises are broken,
the bottle not strong enough to survive the elements—
its shards pummeled
into sea glass,
my words, absorbed by the salt water.
She took the love I tried to send to you.

I try to counter with her—
retrieve my words from her depths,
but she would rather consume me.
My world goes black—
an assault on my senses;
I'm drowning in limitless space,
wrapped in her embrace.
My heartbeat beats wildly in my chest.
I fight to find my breath.
I'm caught beneath the surface
when I hear her say,
If this love is so easily lost,
perhaps it wasn't meant to last.

She releases me from her undertow.
Sea air fills my lungs.
It feels like inhaling for the first time,
and on the exhale, I dispel the weight of you.
My mind is numb when I return to shore—
drenched and disheartened.

The tide recedes,
her message heeded.
And I am
alone again.

The poet made the fool.
That is, until I hear it.
She turned my prose into a Siren song—
my pain into something beautiful.

Love that is deep can never truly be unrequited.
In my solitude, I find solace
in this.

Reach

I am reaching out to you.
Can you feel me?

I'm sorry if it's too much.
I just want you to know I'm here.

I am reduced to a thing that wants.

Payphone

Somewhere along the way,
we got our
     wires
         crossed—
lost in translation.

Dial tones
that never led to an
answering machine.

I might as well be calling from
the last standing payphone in NYC—
disconnected and
stuck behind museum glass.
Preserved for posterity.

I look at us like that—
something to remember fondly.

Butterflies

I want to tell you
that you make me feel butterflies
that hurt my stomach when they settle
because their presence means
I'm getting close to someone again.
And that means the countdown has begun.

See, they're trapped behind my ribcage,
and every day is one closer to their release
because when the rapid pounding of my heart
bursts open my chest,
they're gone.
And I miss them.
But this is really my way of saying—
I anticipate heartbreak so easily that it laces my expectations.
So it's not a matter of if you will leave…
it's when.

I want to tell you
that I don't mind being alone,
but I don't like being
lonely.
And I wish this time you would stay,
but I know, like my butterflies,
you can't be encaged.

This time, I have to set you free.

Coffee Talk

It started with a conversation.
Words flowed like coffee into the cups
we held.

It was easy—
until it wasn't.

I saved you a spot at the table,
but I've been waiting so long that
your coffee's gone cold.

My cup is empty.

Missing Socks

You lost yours in the hotel,
between kisses and gentle touches.
We couldn't find it, but you said
it didn't matter.
A pair became one.

I woke up this morning—
the morning after losing you.
My right sock is missing.
A pair became one.

Difference

There is a logic lost
in love—
an inability for a heart
to see beyond itself
once it has been given over
to another.

I am a rational woman,
yet I have made myself complicit
in my heartbreak,
betrayed by the sincerity of my heart's
desire to love and be loved.

Romantic reciprocity
has long eluded me,
so forgive me for my
rumination.
Perhaps when you arrive
at what you've waited so long to feel,
you cannot accept that you may again
have to go without.

I do not know which is worse—
to remember or to forget,
for both bring pain.
I cannot bring myself to
lay this love to rest.
It seems a contradiction
to end something eternal,
and is that not love when done right?
If I've loved you, part of me always will.

I only wish that my heart would recognize the difference
between its inherent worth and the limits of another's love.
Maybe then I would stop internalizing every ending
as if it were a reflection of what I deserve.
Such objectivity would set me free.

I don't think most people want to be known
as intimately as I desire
to know them.

Phantom

What am I, if not for the warmth
beneath your fingertips?
My words are only heard when you can trace them
on my skin.

The mortality of this body begs for an
earthly anchor,
a connection that will extend beyond
the wants of the flesh.
If I am in your arms, has it anything to
do with me?
Or were you tired of having no one to hold?

I'll play this part just long enough to feel seen,
but the impermanence is killing me.
I'm no more than your phantom
in the night,
singing sweet nothings until the sun rises.

I will try to hold onto you in hopes
that I can make an impression—
leave a mark that maybe you won't
want to scrub away,
but you remove me as easily as you found me;
wipe me from your memory
because to have,
you realize,
is harder than being
alone.

I watch your new beginning, left here,
still holding the weight of
our end.

Honey Glow

I see us in a honey glow,
wrapped in the warmth
of memory,
when everything was new,
and I looked at you and saw forever
at that moment.

You reached for my hand.
"I want to remember this."

When did you stop remembering me?

We're too young to hang on,
but I'm not ready to let go.
Mine is a stubborn heart.

And maybe that's the problem.
I hung on to your words even after
you were long gone.

So tell me, please, how am I supposed
to tell my heart it's over?

Costume Jewelry

I see girls from my hometown
in white dresses,
and it sends me into a spiral.
I wasn't born to be a bride,
but I was made to love.

To each their own timeline.

I talked about forever once
when a stranger mistook my ring
for a diamond.
Put my partner on the spot—

Are you going to marry her?

Such promises should never be rushed,
but then again,
when I asked if we had a future,
the answer was always
Yes.

So I wonder, what does love truly mean
when it's spoken right before
they leave?

An Honest Love

You hold the ghosts of people
I tried hard not to
compete with,
but I tainted our love with
insecurity.

It was all new to me,
but we both made mistakes,
promising tomorrows we won't see
together.

If we were able to verbalize our shortcomings,
could we be more honest in love?
Would we then have the courage to admit,

*"Yes, I love you, but I cannot love you
in the ways that you need."*

If we meet again, will we be strangers after all this time?
Or will it be as strangers that we remain?

10 Years

Maybe you'll be the friend
I see on my Instagram feed
in 10 years.
I'll look at you longingly.
The kind of look you give a first love;
an almost love;
love not given the space
to mature.

Maybe you'll have a wife
and the daughter
you mentioned wanting.
She'll have your hair
and, I'm sure, your sense of humor.
A window into a life
that worked better with your timeline.

There's still time
while this exists as mere conjecture,
and this love is still alive in me.
And it was you who said
our story wasn't over.
But you mustn't give my mind
so much free rein.
It'll write a one-sided ending,
forgetting that if your words held intention,
you'd pick up a pen too.

Wouldn't it be easier if this were fiction?
Then I wouldn't have to face the reality
that, though I want to wait for you,
you're not asking me to stay.

What's in a Name?

What's in a name? That which we call a rose
By any other name would smell as sweet.

Shakespeare talked of family names,
as did my grandmother.
She told me to keep my maiden name,
should I ever choose to marry.

That's who you are, she said.
And I agree.

I don't want a new surname;
I want my name remembered.

Not only men should be tasked
with legacy.

I wanted to be your partner, not your project.

Portia

after William Shakespeare's The Merchant of Venice

"If you do love me, you will find
me out- "

And so you did.
Chose the casket of lead
and thought yourself
a savior.

You wanted me
until the burden of conversation
became a tax.

Put the outcome in my charge
using platitudes—
Said:

"As doubtful whether what I see
be true,
Until confirmed, signed, ratified
by you."

But must we speak with such formality?

Love is no trial to be won—
no home for your
lexicon of litigation.

But if this is the language I must use
to get through to you,
just know you've met
your match.

In borrowed robes,
I own the floor
with my penchant for proverbs—
a Philadelphia lawyer.

My tactic is to try you on technicalities
because something must be said when words
and actions don't agree.

All I required was your love,
Lord B.
The presence of your person.

Never to be positioned to prove
I am your equal.

Pedestal

I'm walking through the gallery,
surrounded by marble bodies.

Sculptors tried to capture the image of gods,
but what if their true intention was to preserve
the essence of their lovers?

How often do we put our loves on pedestals?

I always wanted to see the best in you—
carve your image into stone so I wouldn't forget
what you felt like.

But you've grown cold,
like the marble I chipped at
with every soft word I spoke to you.

Maybe every art museum is a hall
of lost love.

Joan

A woman's intuition
is the poetry of knowing—
the visions that are obvious only
to her soul.
Herein lies her power.

History recounts the dissonance
of this voice when denied.
But it cannot be silenced—
only brought from one life
into the next.

No wonder he called me Joan—
the reincarnation of a rebellious
woman.

Surrounded by war,
clairvoyance became holy counsel
to a young Joan of Arc.
Though she wept when the Saints
wouldn't take her away.
In this, I understand her—
longing to live in a space
untouched by grief.
This is what I have come to name
Love.

She never took a lover,
and perhaps in that way, she was
stronger than I
and my pattern of escaping
into people.

A search for solace
that would have me forget
I have been the constant
in braving my darkest days.

Forever will Joan be the timeless heroine.
A woman whose fierceness led her
to the front lines,
her conviction not shaken
even when struck by an arrow
in battle.
No pain could deter her from
making sure her men
did not retreat.

How telling this is of
a woman's love.
For her, of her country,
and mine of man,
both an opening in our armor that we dare expose,
for I have my puncture wounds to show—
not unscathed by Cupid's arrow.
And just like her, I long for such a simple thing—
for someone to be proud to stand with me.
To not run when fortune fails
to favor us.

Though the odds were stacked against her,
Joan wanted Paris—
the City of Love,
the heart of her country.
It was her first defeat.

Much like her, I lost discernment
when caught in the crossfire
of my desire

and misstepped in the heat of it,
compromising my hold on the heart
of the man I loved.
Maybe he and I should have admitted defeat
when we both had wounds that started to bleed,
but I believed that we
could see our troubles through.

Is it naive to have hope
when trust has been tested?
Or telling of one's faith?
We are all bound by our choices.

Once her victories stopped, Joan fell from good graces,
and the celebrated heroine became
a convicted heretic.
For it was outside the bounds of reason
that she should converse with the Divine.
But even at the cost of her life, she would not recant
the voices of the Saints.
To deny her truth would be nothing more
than a damned existence.

In love, I denied the truth to forgo facing reality
but paid the price of reducing myself
to a lesser life of longing.
One cannot survive on the periphery
of another's love, and pining
is only pretty in poetry.

I wonder if Joan wept when salvation didn't come.
A prayer on her lips before being kissed by death.
Her body was burned three times
because they could not burn her heart.
The protection of a pious soul—
lost too soon and swept into the Seine.

Many will offer up their bodies
before bearing their hearts in
their hands,
but I was not made to love
in pieces.
To let someone learn your heart
is the truest way to have your soul known,
and everything I've sacrificed has been in the name
of being understood.

When my heart was broken,
I watched its remains be returned
as I was called beautiful
while I cried.
I've learned to carry my pain well,
but a resilient heart still bleeds.

I never wanted to rescind the *I Love You*
freely given from my lips,
but something so holy should not be said in vain.
After all, it was I who made myself a martyr
by staying until I became the casualty.

Twenty-five years following her trial,
Joan was absolved of her wrongful conviction,
and her name was later christened as a saint.
Taking her life could not take away her rightful legacy.
So often, the goodness of a woman is only seen in hindsight.

So let my love be my legacy,
an imprint on a shared history
deep enough to outlast me.
It does not have to be returned,
but it is not something to be dismissed.
I am not to be forgotten.

People Change, but Love Remains

Change is the only constant.
I know this all too well,
but I believe it to be more complicated
than that.

We survive multiple deaths throughout our lives—
those of the metaphysical kind.
I've lost versions of people who are
still alive,
and there's no word to describe that ache—
when someone exists in a memory no one else can see.

Maybe we imagine people to be a version of themselves
that never truly existed beyond our gaze.
Could we be so powerful as to create alternate identities
for those we most love?

Perhaps that's just the nature of our influence on one another.
When lives become intertwined, they change each other irrevocably.
All we can do is hope we continue to grow in sync,
though cruelty comes from knowing this isn't always the case.
We always think we have forever
before reality humbles us.

I know you don't understand why it's hard for me to forget—
why I preserve moments in ink to hold onto old feelings.
But I just think if someone matters to you,
that shouldn't need an explanation.

So I hold this as true, even as I say goodbye.
The past is a distant memory I can recall with fondness,
but it no longer has a pulse.

To love, is poetry personified,
eloquence in motion.
And even when it isn't enough,
it still matters.
It always will.

Wounds

It's fascinating—
the fixation we have on our pain;
the ways we replay the hurt
instead of letting it heal.
As if keeping it alive
will prevent it from happening again.

I'd never been in love before I met you,
but I was carrying the criticisms
of people I had tried to.
And with just your words,
you sutured those wounds.
So when the scars began to form,
I put my trust in you.
Never did I imagine the damage
that would do.

You let me believe I could be loved in my softness.
Let me bare the underbelly
of my soul,
only for you to sink your teeth in,
reopening those scars that formed but never faded,
leaving me to lick wounds
made worse by your knowledge of them.

But then again, pain changed us both.

I cannot say I am blameless when I know
I left you bruised.
I put my unprocessed pain on you and made you
remember old wounds.
I hope you don't resent me for it.

Say you won't wear me as a wound,
and I promise to not hold this hurt
against you.

Forgiveness is a salve when followed through.
So let us remove one another
from the connotations of our choices,
because we don't have to accept mistreatment as truth.

It only cut this deep because you loved me,
and I loved you.

Lessons in Love

My hand on your back
in a Brooklyn bar
and the way you looked at me.
It felt like being found
after months of not feeling seen.
But that was the beginning of the reaching.

Damn the damsel in distress,
but maybe part of me did seek saving.
I desired freedom and mistook it in your face;
cupped your cheek in my hand
and called you mine,
because what do we reach for when we feel alone,
if not love?

You had me from the moment you called me poetry,
but the way I fell came from a deeper need.
Yours is a diplomatic mind,
and I was searching for solid ground.
So with every conversation,
you slowly became my synonym for safety.

Freshly sprung from a season in hell,
I was still removed from my sense of self,
and you mirrored the parts of me I needed to see.
An admiration that extended both ways, as I saw in you
a boldness I craved.

But I became blind to the fine line between
admiration and comparison,
failing to catch when I made you
a metric I measured myself against.

I only realized the cost of reaching for your recognition
when you called me that final time,
and the lie that I was fine could no longer cover the truth.
Too attached to what you represented,
my fear of what I was
losing in you
overshadowed what had already been
lost in me.
Love should not take more than it gives,
yet I had nothing left.

Though I wish it hadn't happened,
love lacerated me to let the light in,
and you became my lesson.
I finally realized that the parts of you I reached for
were the parts of me that have not yet had
the same space to breathe.
So I'll bless the breaking rather than curse the pain,
for it forced me to shift my focus back to me.

No love is perfect, and I know I gave you a lot to carry,
but the comfort of your kindness
reminded me of my strength.
Now I know I can hold myself from here.

Roses

The roses were pink
that October
in New York.

We chased the foliage
across
      state
            lines,
and that's when you learned
that as long as we were together,
you'd never want for vibrancy.

I loved you in high definition.
It wasn't perfect,
I know.
But it was the best I knew how.

You took my picture set against the flowers.
A snapshot of happiness,
a memento of that which was
destined to fade.

Because the roses weren't winterized.
The frost wasn't forgiving.
The petals wilted in November,
and by December,
they were gone.

I know you see me in the flower beds.
That's not a bad way to be
remembered—
in something beautiful.

The buds are returning,
and soon the roses will bloom
again.

I hope we each find happiness
in this new season.

Sacred Love

Sometimes love has made me feel
as though I am unworthy—
that I have asked too much,
that to want is wrong.
And I want for so much.

I have known satisfaction, but it has been fleeting.
The arms that have held me in my softness,
the touch I called home,
the affirmations of love I waited so long to hear—
they have all faded.

I ask only from love what I am willing to give,
which is to say, if I love you, I will give you the world—
my world.
To open my life and soul with the hope,
the *expectation*,
that you will not turn your back on me;
that you will hold me in the blanket of sanctity
I deserve.

I think that we must expect to live in the fullness of love.
I reject the idea that this is too big of an ask.
How could wanting to be loved ever be wrong?

To have an open heart in a guarded world is sometimes painful,
but there is peace beyond pain.
I have seen glimpses of love's holiness,
but only after daring to be vulnerable.

When we are willing to surrender, love reveals its ease.
I will never chide my heart for continuing to believe in a sacred love.

Those I have loved have brought me closer to the truth of who I am.
In that way, nothing has been lost, only gained.

A Lost Love is Still Love

May I speak to this year like a love that knew me
in my most intimate moments,
but understood that our story was
a chapter
rather than
forever.

When we began our rendezvous,
I didn't know what I didn't know.
I found growth in the unearthing of feelings
buried deep within my soul.
I revere every laugh, every tear, and every smile
gifted in the breaking down of the person
I thought I was.

There is intimacy in allowing the possibility of heartbreak, after all.
Maybe that's why the close of each year
carries an unspoken sadness.

So let me pass it with grace.
A lost love is still love.
Let the lessons linger on my tongue,
in hopes I might share them with you—
the New Year.

I come to you stronger and more sure.
My wounded heart is an offering of
unconditional love.
Proof that despite my scars,
it is still beating.

I will knock to the tune of "Auld Lang Syne"
as I arrive at your door with open arms.
Please take me as I am.
I have fought so hard to get here.

I'll speak to you like a newfound love
because, when the clock strikes twelve,
we begin writing this next chapter
together.

Unapologetic

I have a bad habit
of trying to guess what everyone thinks of me.
But I am tired of living in the shadow
of imagined opinions
when I would much rather bask in the glow of
unapologetic truth.

That is to say,
I'm done over-explaining myself.
I'm ready to just be.

Your opinion of me is really
none of my business.
But I can't say I'm not happy that
I cross your mind.

I have been told that I think, feel, and love
too much.
It's a scary phenomenon to be on the receiving end of.
But is that not the best compliment?
My being cannot be contained.
I am overflowing from my cup,
and inviting you in to share
the holy magic of it all.

So tell me, do you consider it a sin to think yourself divine?

If you don't stoke your fire,
someone is bound to come along
and extinguish it.
I hope you never give them that power.

I once longed to hear "*I love you*"
echo on someone else's lips,
maybe for a lack of self-love.

But the meaning of those three words
is dulled when you can't
repeat them to your reflection.

It's not egotistical to be your own #1 fan.
And if it is, why not be a bit selfish?

I've learned that ignoring my intuition
only hurts me in the end.
So I'm no longer accepting anyone else's word
as gospel—
no longer using others
as my mirror.

I don't need to walk through this life quietly
in fear that my breath won't sync with yours—
that my being will upset
the balance.

I have the audacity to fill the room now.
I will no longer apologize myself away—
no longer shrink myself in the name of someone
else's comfort.

If I'm to be known in any way,
I hope it's for daring to live my life boldly,
no matter how that looks from the outside.

So yes, I am intense…
And I like it that way.

I will love you so deeply
that it will probably scare you away.
But I don't regret a minute of it.
What a gift it is to fully embody my feelings!

I'll continue to think too much
about everything
because that's the key to unlocking
the worlds that exist inside me.

I have a hunger for the fulfillment of my dreams,
so I'll go on, following where my passion leads.

After all, my desire is holy.

If I'm too much,
no one is asking you to stay.

My only priority is living my
life for me.

Sun Shower

I am like a sun shower—
a paradoxical duet.
Two things that shouldn't exist to
complement one another,
yet they do.
A combination of the desired and undesirable.

Ignore the one,
and perhaps you can still
appreciate the beauty of the preferred.
Enjoy the warmth on your face and pretend
the droplets don't roll off your skin—
cold and unpleasant.
But maybe that's a glass-half-empty mentality
because I still believe in those who love to
sing in the rain.

When I say that I'm like a
sun shower,
I'm not lesser due to one,
but a harmony of dissonance.
Two things that, together,
are a lot more interesting than
alone
because they aren't "supposed" to work in tandem.
But when they do,
they cause you to stop and notice.

And I'd rather be out of the ordinary
than be one of the same.

Wild Woman

My lineage is rooted in the soil
of the Carpathian Mountains:
Lemkovyna.
Home to the Lemko people—
a people exiled from the land
they tilled for generations.
So I wonder, is it in my DNA to long for places
I can never return to?

I feel more at home in the paintings of
Romantics—
those of ethereal beauty.
That which critiques how far we've removed ourselves
from all that is natural,
in the name of progress.

I remember my humanity most when I'm one with
Mother Earth.

Sometimes when I look at a sunset-laden sky
I think of which paints I would mix
to capture the correct colors.
I think this is how I must be loved.
I need someone to look at me and have the desire
to know what I am made of.

Find me in nature's palette:
sensation, sight, and sound.
I'll be the breeze at the break of dawn
when the heat of summer cools,
waking you gently.
The rouge to autumn's painted leaves,
beckoning a cycle of seasons—a reminder

that we must let go to move forward.
But oh, how beautiful that can be.
And when winter's shadow descends,
I'll be the comfortable silence of the falling snow,
enveloping you in peace—
a promise that spring's renewal is never far away,
and soon you will be waking to the serenade of birdsong.

Now you see the rhythm—
the pulse of this life, too often hidden by our focus on
things that time will name trivial.

These days, I am trying to slow my pace
to sync with this remembering.

An ode to my roots—
Lemkovyna.

We are a people of the land,
and when I die,
I will return to the soil.
My body will fade with the seasons,
the flowers will entomb me.
Let the roses cover me until their briars
grow to protect my soul.

Only then will there no longer be a need for metaphor.
I may at last be one with all that I find beautiful
in this life.

After all, I was always a wild woman.

Female Divinity

If trauma is carried in the body,
I am the embodiment of every woman who
came before me.
Every forced hand in marriage,
every rape disguised as duty,
every "*Sit still and shut up.*"

If trauma is carried in the body,
my heartbeat is the echo of
every heart song thrashed,
every spike from fear, and
every lull before death.

But if trauma is carried in the body,
I am a warrior,
conceding no more of myself than is necessary
for survival.
I am a goddess incarnate,
a body to be worshiped because I can carry
the weight of their pain
and mine.

I am my ancestors' legacy.
A mirror of themselves,
I hope, makes them proud.
I am the face of female divinity,
blessed and cursed by my sex.
I am theirs, but more importantly,
I am mine.

The pain molded me,
but it does not define me.
Their lives were not lived in vain,
and neither shall mine be.

My Body Belongs to Nobody

Weight:
a descriptor so variable as to be
meaningless.
Why, then, have I been told that I am worth
more
when that number is
less?

I remember the first time I started to see my body
as something to critique.
The mirror became an enemy—
my reflection, the instigator.
It suddenly became more comfortable to
hide beneath sweaters and
behind dark colors.
Anything to make me feel like I was taking up less space.

But is that not the message we often receive as women?
Just
be
less.

But for who?
My view of my body was a warped perception
planted by a society intent on policing it.
Though they're so stealthy
and I was too young.

Too young to see that the beauty I was chasing
was killing me
and that it's not normal to live in
a perpetual state of hunger—
hungering for an image of myself that would satiate
everyone else's cravings
but leave me wanting.

Tell me, where is the satisfaction
in watching a young girl pick herself apart?
I didn't know how
to block out the noise.
That's what the commentary always was.

When you're conditioned to see your body
through the lens of others' opinions,
you lose sight of your voice,
replaced by a longing for approval.

But what happens when that wound doesn't heal?

I saw the conversation shift from anatomy to sexuality.
My body was torn apart only to be put on a pedestal,
now an object of desire.

My body belongs to nobody.
But that doesn't stop people from trying to
own what isn't theirs.

They say that your body is a temple,
but there was a time when I found no solace in mine.
A place I could no longer bear to be
after uninvited hands
took liberties.

Attraction is not a synonym for consent.

I think most people objectify beauty.
But I refuse to be the casualty.
I concede none of my autonomy.
I refuse to exist merely as a thing to please.

I am a vessel for beautiful things.
Thoughts spring forth from the tip of my tongue,
and you should not be surprised that
beauty and intellect are not
mutually exclusive.
There's power in my opinions
if you'd care enough
to listen,
but I don't need your audience;
I'm taking the stage regardless.
I'm not asking permission anymore.

But I will ask you this:

What conversations are you having with your daughters?
And why are they so different from those with your sons?
I don't want to be approached with cautionary tales
when he's told that the world is his for the taking
because you see what planting that seed can do.

Giving is not a condition of womanhood,
yet you'd be fooled into thinking it is.
We are expected to give of our time,
our love, and
our bodies
because sacrifice is applauded when
you're a woman.
Give everything until you feel like nothing.

But now I'm taking action.
Let this be a call for reclamation.
Take back your power from all who ever made
you feel powerless.

Take

Up

Space.

I'm still learning how to
uncage myself
from the prison of criticism,
but on the days I'm able to look at my
reflection in the mirror
and feel pride
rather than shame—
the days I don't pick myself apart,
don't beg to be loved—
I know I'm healing.
Step by step.

I forgive myself for making my body the enemy
and for not standing in my power.
Forget wedding vows:
In sickness and in health,
is my pledge to myself.

Nobody loves me like my body.

Antithetical Anthem

Lately, I've become the most
pessimistic optimist,
which is to say,
I'm a constant contradiction,
and the things that once seemed easy
feel like they've become complex
overnight.

I find myself in an endless cycle of
mourning the old me's,
but maybe that just means I'm paying attention.
After all, I've become a master at introspection—
my superpower and my kryptonite.

But the changes have become harder to describe—
feelings that have not yet been named—
and all I want is for you to understand.
So I'll sing the Antithetical Anthem of Youth,
hoping maybe I can order my chaos;
hoping maybe my metaphors will make sense
to you.

My life looks different than how I thought it would,
but maybe that idea was always a rough sketch.
I've spilt the paint cans,
blurred all the lines,
and sometimes it feels like I'm constantly working
from a fresh page—
that I can't seem to finish the picture.
But then I remember that we're all just works in progress, and

every iteration is built on experience.
So I'll erase the notion that this
is a return to square one.
At least, I'll try.

I use comparison like a vice,
still finding myself in the cracks
of the façade I've fashioned to be liked.
Recovering people pleaser,
but some habits die hard.
So when my friends are doing shots at the bar
while I drink wine from
a plastic cup,
my mind frames it as a metaphor for
things that don't belong.

I worry that I'm not the first choice,
and I'm tired of not being chosen.
I have wedding invites arriving in the mail,
but I've yet to know the permanence of a person.
I'm not ready for forever,
but my heart is capable of a love that is.
Maybe therein lies the dissonance.
I promise I'll be the best love affair,
and maybe next time someone will want to
stay.

Feeling lonely doesn't mean I'm alone, though,
because my friends are the fiercest.
They helped me through heartbreak,
validating every feeling
while I processed my mistakes.

That's the blessing of best friends.
They never let you
lack in love.

So I carry their message that
I am enough,
correcting patterns of self-effacing thinking
because I know I put everyone else on a pedestal
to not have my confidence mistaken for ego.
But I have a right to be celebrated too.

Trusting myself is sometimes trying
when I feel the pressures of a predetermined checklist:
career, spouse, house.
The things we use as general markers for progress.

And isn't it exhausting to carry
the weight of years
in a day?
Yes.
But I do it anyway.

Passionately impatient,
I'm made defensive
when approached more with the question,
What do you do? rather than, *How are you?*
Because if I can't quantify my value, it's like it doesn't exist.
So tell me, what's the price of a life well lived?

I've been praised for my potential,
but potential feels taunting.
It feels like being the "almost" in every sentence—

the thing never realized.
And if I can never reach the summit,
what good is this path I'm on?

This is what we don't talk about.
Sometimes your circumstances are
not for a lack of trying,
and we all deserve a little more credit.
I give everyone and everything my best,
but there are still people who try to sell me
on my unworthiness.

So when the world starts to feel like
a fishbowl I'm staring out of,
half removed,
I have to remind myself that burnout exists.
And here I am, in the thick of it.
The consequence of constantly being put
in a position to prove my worth.

Just for a moment, I'd like to slow down—
sit in the unknown without trying to define the undefinable.
Constantly, I'm pushing the needle for everyone else
because I've always been so mature for my age.
Can I just be happy here for a minute?
Breathe in sync with the rhythm of my life's timeline
instead of losing my breath to keep up with yours.
I don't have a 10-year plan, but that doesn't mean
I'm without vision.
I'm answering the call of my ambition, and
some things just can't be seen on the surface.

So the next time someone passively dismisses my passions
or sees me as something that needs to be fixed,
I won't listen.
I won't let the criticisms seep in before I can acknowledge
that there are compliments too.
I'll stand proud in my conviction to stay true to the things
that are uniquely me.
This is the price of a life well lived.

And should you decide to ask, *How are you?*
I've already given you my answer.
Acknowledged both sides of the coin
and then flipped it to change my perspective.

Multiple truths can exist, and that's not
duplicitous.
So it should come as no surprise
that I'm not easily
summarized.
Nor do I want to be,
because living to meet someone else's
standards only creates a false
sense of security.

My success is self-defined, and
by my measure, I'm doing fine.

Acknowledgments

To be an artist, in any form, is to accept vulnerability—
to allow the world to see you through your work and form
their opinions. It is gratifying and nerve-racking, requiring
self-assurance and a strong support system for moments of
wavering confidence. Writing this book was no exception. It
was a project that challenged me to overcome my inner critic
to create from a place of authenticity—a process that required
all of me. This relationship with my art is one that my friends
and family know well, and it is them I'd like to thank for their
encouragement while working on this book.

To my friends, thank you for being my biggest cheerlead-
ers. You recognized how important this book is to me and
celebrated every stage of my writing process, easing my doubts
and anxieties along the way. Your continued interest in my

work was the motivation I needed, and it truly made me feel so loved. You are all lights in my life, and I'm so grateful to have you in my corner.

To my Mom, Dad, and sister, Faith, thank you for believing in me. This book was at the forefront of many of our conversations over the past year, and I appreciate the care you took in helping me revise my work. More importantly, you reminded me that my stories are worth telling and encouraged me to use my voice. I love you.

And finally, to those of you reading this, thank you for choosing to spend your time within these pages. I hope this book can serve as a space to feel without judgment—to honor the range of emotions that come with living fully alive.

About the Author

A DYNAMIC STORYTELLER, KARA DOBIAS has honored her need for creative expression by working across mediums. In addition to being a poet, she is a classically trained operatic soprano, actress, and dancer with a degree in Theatre Arts from Drew University. For her, creativity is a way of life—a continuous journey of self-discovery and a means to connect with the world around her. In her debut poetry book, *Alive*, she explores how metaphor can act as medicine, helping us to hold a mirror to ourselves. Through her work, she hopes to leave an imprint that resonates with authenticity and speaks to our shared humanity.

For more of her work, visit karadobias.com or connect with her on Instagram @karadobias